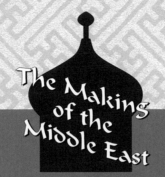

The Making of the Middle East

# The First World War and the End of the Ottoman Order

The Making of the Middle East

# The First World War and the End of the Ottoman Order

Kristine Brennan

Mason Crest Publishers
Philadelphia

Frontis: The Hagia Sophia was a famous symbol of Ottoman power. Once a Christian cathedral, it was converted to a mosque after the Ottoman army captured Constantinople in 1453.

Produced by OTTN Publishing, Stockton, N.J.

**Mason Crest Publishers**
370 Reed Road
Broomall, PA 19008
www.masoncrest.com

First printing

1  3  5  7  9  8  6  4  2

Library of Congress Cataloging-in-Publication Data

Brennan, Kristine, 1969-
  The First World War and the End of the Ottoman Order / Kristine Brennan.
      p. cm. — (The making of the Middle East)
  Includes bibliographical references and index.
  ISBN-13: 978-1-4222-0168-8
  ISBN-10: 1-4222-0168-6
  1.  World War, 1914-1918—Turkey. 2.  Turkey—History—20th century. 3.  Turkey—History—
Ottoman Empire, 1288-1918.  I. Title.
  D566.B74 2007
  940.3'56—dc22
                                   2007024552

Arab-Israeli Relations, 1950–1979

The Arabian Peninsula in the Age of Oil

The Cold War in the Middle East, 1950–1991

The Iranian Revolution and the Resurgence of Islam

The Middle East in the Age of Uncertainty, 1991–Present

The Ottoman and Qajar Empires in the Age of Reform

The Palestine Mandate and the Creation of Israel, 1920–1949

The Rise of Nationalism: The Arab World, Turkey, and Iran

Tensions in the Gulf, 1978–1991

# Table of Contents

# Introduction:
# The Importance of the Middle East

The region known as the Middle East has a significant impact on world affairs. The countries of the greater Middle East—the Arab states of the Arabian Peninsula, Eastern Mediterranean, and North Africa, along with Israel, Turkey, Iran, and Afghanistan—possess a large portion of the world's oil, a valuable commodity that is the key to modern economies. The region also gave birth to three of the world's major faiths: Judaism, Christianity, and Islam.

In recent years it has become obvious that events in the Middle East affect the security and prosperity of the rest of the world. But although such issues as the wars in Iraq and Afghanistan, the floundering Israeli-Palestinian peace process, and the struggles within countries like Lebanon and Sudan are often in the news, few Americans understand the turbulent history of this region.

Human civilization in the Middle East dates back more than 8,000 years, but in many cases the modern conflicts and issues in the region can be attributed to events and decisions made during the past 150 years. In particular, after World War I ended in 1918, the victorious Allies—especially France and Great Britain—redrew the map of the Middle East, creating a number of new countries, such as Iraq, Jordan, and Syria. Other states, such as Egypt and Iran, were dominated by foreign powers until after the Second World War. Many of the Middle Eastern countries did not become independent until the 1960s or 1970s. Political and economic developments in the Middle Eastern states over the past four decades have shaped the region's direction and led to today's headlines.

The purpose of the MAKING OF THE MIDDLE EAST series is to nurture a better understanding of this critical region, by providing the basic history along

with explanation and analysis of trends, decisions, and events. Books will examine important movements in the Middle East, such as the development of nationalism in the 1880s and the rise of Islamism from the 1970s to the present day.

The 10 volumes in the MAKING OF THE MIDDLE EAST series are written in clear, accessible prose and are illustrated with numerous historical photos and maps. The series should spark students' interest, providing future decision-makers with a solid foundation for understanding an area of critical importance to the United States and the world.

(Right) David Lloyd George of Britain, Vittorio Orlando of Italy, Georges Clemenceau of France, and Woodrow Wilson of the United States confer outside a hotel during the Paris Peace Conference, 1919. At the conference the Allies agreed to break up the Ottoman Empire. (Opposite) Istanbul's ancient fortifications overlook the Bosporus strait, a critical waterway in the region.

# 1 *An Unacceptable Peace*

In April 1920, 10 months after Germany signed the Treaty of Versailles to end World War I, representatives from Great Britain, France, Italy, and other Allied powers met at San Remo, a city on the Mediterranean coast of Italy. The diplomats were gathered primarily to discuss the provisions of the Versailles peace treaty, particularly how the defeated Ottoman Empire, which had fought alongside Germany and Austria-Hungary during the war, would be divided among the Allied powers.

At the war's outset, the Ottoman Empire stretched over most of the region known as the Middle East, including present-day Turkey as well as the Eastern Mediterranean region and parts of the Arabian Peninsula. Much of this territory was captured by Allied troops during the conflict, and after the

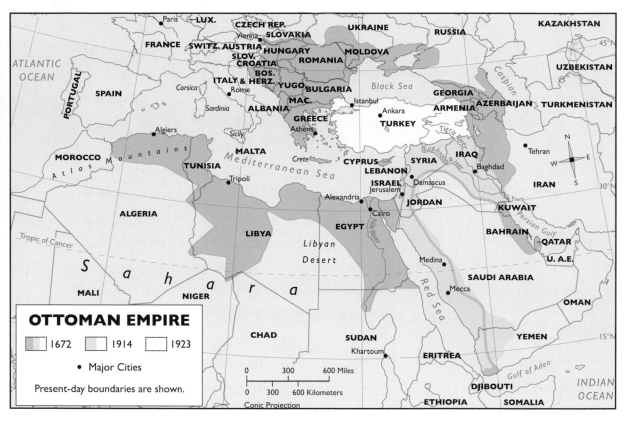

**OTTOMAN EMPIRE**

▨ 1672　▨ 1914　☐ 1923

• Major Cities

Present-day boundaries are shown.

This map shows the borders of the Ottoman Empire at various periods. The 17th century marked the empire's greatest size, with the Ottoman sultan ruling a vast area of Eastern Europe, North Africa, the Caucasus, and the Middle East. However, by the start of World War I in 1914 the empire had been stripped of much of its territory.

war the Allied governments were anxious to divide up the spoils of their victory. They were so intent on parceling up Ottoman land that the Allies did not bother to invite representatives from the Ottoman territories to San Remo to help decide the region's future.

Shut out of discussions concerning their post-war fate, the fainthearted Ottoman ruler, Sultan Mehmed VI, did his best to show the Allies that he would cooperate with whatever plans they had for reorganizing the empire. To prove his willing compliance, the sultan shut down his parliament and demobilized the Ottoman army. Residents of the empire struggled with food shortages and disease. A British commissioner took over government decision-making, and Allied troops occupied Istanbul and other important cities.

In August 1920 the sultan's government sent four representatives to France to conclude the Treaty of Sevres, a formal peace agreement with the Allies. Its terms included relinquishing control over all non-Turkish lands. Most of these parts of the former empire were turned into small new countries that would be administered by Allied governments under the authority of the League of Nations. The Treaty of Sevres called for the Great Britain to take control of Mesopotamia and Palestine. France would oversee the affairs of Lebanon and Syria. The Italians, who had already occupied parts of Southern Anatolia, the Dodecanese Islands, and Rhodes since defeating the Ottoman army in 1911, would occupy those territories permanently. Thrace and Western Anatolia would be given to Greece.

The concession to Greece was particularly galling to the Turks, because Greece had long contested Ottoman control over the strategic waterways connecting the Black Sea and the Aegean Sea. The Bosporus and Dardanelles

A representative of the Ottoman sultan arrives at Sevres to sign a treaty with the Allies, 1920. The humiliating Treaty of Sevres would have reduced Ottoman territory to an area smaller than the modern state of Turkey.

straits and the Sea of Marmara, which lay between them, would no longer be under Ottoman control. Possession of the straits was what had made the Ottoman capital Istanbul so important in international trade for centuries. The straits were also of great military importance, although this mattered little to the sultan after the treaty stripped his military force and reduced his standing army to no more than 50,000 soldiers.

When the sultan's weak government signed the Treaty of Sevres on August 10, 1920, only a fraction of the old Ottoman Empire was left, and it was hemmed in on all sides by more powerful nations. Istanbul was occupied by Allied soldiers, and the sultan had little power to govern even the Turkish lands. However, Turks who were dissatisfied with the Allied occupation formed a nationalist movement in Ankara, a city which lies about 200 miles southeast of Istanbul. The leader of the nationalists was an Ottoman war hero named Mustafa Kemal. He and his followers proclaimed that they resisted foreign domination in the name of the sultan, but they had no intention of seeing the old aristocracy returned. Instead, the nationalists wanted to transform the remains of the Ottoman Empire into a strong, modern republic with the power to govern itself and determine its own future.

Calling on all Turkish people to obey the orders of his Representative Committee in Ankara, Mustafa Kemal encouraged a general resistance campaign against the British, French, Italian, and Greek occupiers. He formed a new parliament (called the Grand National Assembly) that quickly elected him its new president. Though he had popular support, Kemal had limited supplies and no coordinated military command to fight against the Allies. Over the next two years, he and the nationalists would have to create an army, negotiate with foreign powers for weapons and aid, and fight to regain control of their land.

For more than 500 years, the Ottoman Empire was one of the world's great powers. (Opposite) The army of Sultan Mehmed II attacks Constantinople, 1453. After the Turks captured the ancient capital of the Roman Empire, the sultan renamed the city Istanbul. (Right) The feared Turkish cavalry rides into battle.

# 2 *A Proud Heritage*

The Ottoman Empire derives its name from its first leader, Osman (born A.D. 1258), who established a kingdom in Anatolia, the part of present-day Turkey that lies in Asia Minor. In the first years of the 14th century, Osman began organizing nomadic Turkish tribes into a united fighting force. With the stated intention of spreading Islam, the majority religion of the Turkish nomads, Osman began subjugating Anatolian tribes and waging wars against Christian armies in the region. In the 1320s, Osman's warriors even conquered parts of the Balkan nations in Europe, but he was never successful in taking the city of Constantinople, a remnant of the Byzantine Empire that was both a Christian capital and the center of trade between Europe and Asia.

For centuries Constantinople had dominated the waterways between the Black Sea and the Mediterranean, as well as the trade routes between Anatolia and Thrace (the Balkan Peninsula under Ottoman control). The once-powerful Byzantine Empire, successor to the Roman Empire that had fallen in the fifth century, had been weakened by a series of incompetent leaders and constant attacks by nomadic tribes intent on looting its wealth. Although Osman was unable to capture Constantinople, Ottoman troops commanded by his descendant Sultan Mehmed II conquered the city in 1453. Mehmed soon renamed the city Istanbul, and showed his allegiance to Islam by converting the city's famous Christian church, called the Hagia Sophia, into a mosque.

## Religious Tolerance

By 1462 Mehmed's efforts to build up the Muslim population in Istanbul began to bear fruit. The city became a center of Turkish culture and learning. He built mosques and schools (*madrassas*) to spread Islamic teachings. Although Mehmed was a multilingual ruler who kept up on current events, the Europeans he met considered him—and the Turkish people in general—coarse and barbaric. Few Europeans knew how to react to the conquerors. Europeans feared the Turks because they were fierce fighters who had crushed the remnants of the Byzantine Empire, but they were also fascinated by the Turks because of their distinctly non-Western appearance and customs, as well as their unusual trade goods.

Some Christians living in lands conquered by the Ottomans did not consider the Turks to be oppressive masters. In fact, many historians believe that one reason the Ottoman Empire did not suffer disruptive civil strife was because the sultans did not force religious conversion on the peoples they conquered. Although Christians and Jews living in the empire had to pay heavy taxes and pledge loyalty to the sultan, they were generally allowed to practice their beliefs. This religious freedom earned early sultans the loyalty of Orthodox Christians, who found safety in the Ottoman Empire from persecution by Roman Catholics in Europe.

## Expanding Frontiers

In the century after Mehmed's conquest of Constantinople, the Ottoman empire expanded in several directions. During Mehmed's 29-year reign, his armies captured Greece, Trebizond (a Greek state that was a remnant of the Byzantine Empire), and the Crimea (the peninsula between the Black Sea and the Sea of Azov). His son Bayazed II (ruled 1481–1512) had a less eventful reign, as he tried but failed to centralize the empire's power in Istanbul. Bayazed's son Selim I (ruled 1512–1520) overthrew his father. He waged war against another Muslim kingdom, the Mamluk Sultanate to the south, and after a successful campaign Selim I defeated the Mamluks and added Syria, Palestine, and Egypt to his kingdom in 1517. Two important fruits of his conquest were the Islamic holy cities of Mecca and Medina on the Arabian Peninsula, which fell under Ottoman control when the Mamluk Sultanate collapsed.

Selim I's aggressive drive to enlarge the Ottoman Empire set the stage for the reign of Sultan Suleiman I (ruled 1520–1566), who took power at the

Under Sultan Suleiman I (1494–1566), the Ottoman Empire expanded into Eastern Europe and the Middle East. His 46-year reign—the longest in Ottoman history—is regarded as the empire's golden age.

age of 26. Under his rule the empire achieved its greatest glory, as Suleiman's armies conquered the Mediterranean island of Rhodes, much of North Africa, and parts of Persia, the Arabian Peninsula, and Central Europe. The Ottoman armies' advance into Europe was halted at the gates of Vienna. Suleiman's expansion of the empire and his great patronage of the arts, building projects, and legal and educational reform earned him the nickname "the Magnificent" in the West.

By the time Suleiman I died, the Ottoman Empire was one of the world's largest and most powerful empires. At its height, the Ottoman Empire stretched from Anatolia (the Asian part of present-day Turkey) and the Caucasus (mountainous territory between the Black and Caspian Seas), across northern Africa and into Syria, Arabia, and Persia. However, most of the leaders who followed Suleiman were ineffective or incompetent, turning management of the state over to government officials called viziers so that they could pursue their pleasures. Although the Ottoman Empire

A series of weak and ineffective sultans followed Suleiman, and many later rulers misspent public funds to build palaces and monuments rather than investing to strengthen the empire's military or economy. This is the Ishak Pasha Palace, built in the late 17th century in eastern Turkey.

continued to expand for another century, and would remain powerful until the 19th century, widespread corruption contributed to its decay.

## Financial Problems in the Empire

The lavish lifestyles enjoyed by the pleasure-loving sultans, who often used public funds to build new palaces and monuments dedicated to themselves, were a drain on taxpayers, but they were just a small part of the Ottoman Empire's money problems. The sultan's court was often filled with hangers-on who commonly received royal stipends for doing very little. Much of the empire's income was wasted and never went to fund public works or other projects that would help the empire grow.

The Ottoman treasuries also lost potential revenues through the practice of Capitulations, contracts between the empire and European nations giving Europeans living on Ottoman land special privileges and relief from tariffs. The practice had begun in the 1600s, and European merchants were quick to take advantage of their tax-exempt status, selling imported wares at a substantial profit and exporting Ottoman goods at cheap prices. Ottoman merchants found it difficult to compete with European sellers who were granted such trade advantages, and this slowed the native economy.

A gold Ottoman coin minted at Istanbul, 1478. By the 18th century the Ottoman sultans had grown dependent on loans from European powers to maintain their lavish lifestyles.

Furthermore, the sultans found it easy to borrow money from European monarchs and merchant guilds in times of need. Over time the imperial debts grew, until a financial disaster in Europe in 1873 stopped the flow of loans to the empire. By 1874, more than half of the Ottoman Empire's annual budget was earmarked to pay off debts to other countries, and it could borrow no more. Faced with unpayable debts, the Ottoman government narrowly avoided bankruptcy by promising its European lenders that it would establish a financial council to manage repayments. Although within a quarter of a century the debt was under control, this effectively meant that foreign powers were able to exercise a measure of financial authority over the empire.

## Military Weakness

In part because of their financial weakness, the sultans found themselves unable to oppose the encroachment of European powers into territories that had once been part of the empire. Gradually during the 18th and 19th centuries lands at the fringes of the empire were chipped away.

One of the reasons was that by the late 17th century the once-feared Ottoman army was no longer superior to the armies of European states. Typically, Ottoman viziers, who were appointed to their political posts by the sultan, often served as the leaders of military campaigns. This sometimes created problems due to their inexperience or incompetence. Furthermore, the Ottomans were often at a disadvantage because their weapons and tactics were not as good as those used by the Europeans. Ottoman foot soldiers did not drill in set formations the way Europeans did, which made them less disciplined in small-unit engagements. The usual strategy was for a large

Ottoman force to try to overwhelm the enemy with sheer numbers. As their European opponents began to arrange tactics based on improvements in technology and the coordination of various elements of the armed forces (foot soldiers, cavalry, and artillery), the Ottoman forces lagged behind on the battlefield. Muskets and bayonets kept the once-proud Ottoman cavalry at bay and cannon decimated the traditional massed attacks favored by Ottoman leaders.

In 1683 Ottoman grand vizier Kara Mustafa Pasha led a large Ottoman army to the gates of Vienna, hoping to capture the prize that had evaded Suleiman the Magnificent more than a century earlier. Austrian Emperor Leopold II asked neighboring countries for aid in resisting the Turks; his call was answered by King John Sobieski of Poland, who led a force of about 70,000 Germans, Poles, and Austrians to help defend the city. Although the Ottoman army succeeded in breaching the outer walls,

A large bronze cannon stands in front of a painting showing the commander of the Turkish garrison in Belgrade surrendering to Prince Eugene of Savoy. Austria continued to chip away at Ottoman territories in Eastern Europe during the 18th century.

it was unable to exploit this success, and incompetence by Mustafa Pasha led to a crushing defeat.

In 1697 Sultan Mustafa II (ruled 1695–1703) tried to restore Ottoman glory by staging another campaign into Hungary. While attempting to cross the Tisza River on the night of September 11, the Ottomans were taken by surprise by a Hapsburg army under Prince Eugene of Savoy. Thousands of Ottoman troops were slaughtered or drowned in the river while trying to escape.

In 1699, after negotiations facilitated by England and the Netherlands, the Ottoman sultan signed the Treaty of Karlowitz. The next year, the Treaty of Constantinople was signed. These two treaties ended the Austro-Ottoman War of 1683–1697 and turned Hungary and other Slavic territories that had been under Ottoman control over to Austria and Poland. This marked the consolidation of Hapsburg power over much of Central and Eastern Europe and signaled the decline of Ottoman influence in the region.

## Failure to Modernize

The sultans and their representatives were disdainful of European culture, and gave little notice to developments in science, literature, and music. Ottoman isolationism became a problem as the Industrial Revolution took hold in Europe, and the increased trade and manufacturing that industrialization allowed enabled European economies to grow. Although a few sultans took interest in railroads and improved armaments, for the most part they never embraced the promise of an industrial economy. The stage was set for military and political woes that would lead to the downfall of the empire.

(Opposite) Ships pass through the Suez Canal, 1880s. The British took control of Egypt from the Ottomans in 1882 in order to protect the Suez Canal, a critical lifeline to British India. (Right) Mehmed Talat was among the most important leaders of the Young Turk movement in the early 20th century.

# 3 The "Sick Man" of Europe

In 1853 Czar Nicholas I of Russia was talking to Sir George Hamilton Seymour, a British ambassador, about the state of the Ottoman Empire. "We have on our hands a sick man," he is famously quoted as saying, "a very sick man." The "Sick Man of Europe" became a metaphor for the struggling empire that had lost so much territory in warfare and had come increasingly under the influence of foreign powers. By the middle of the 19th century, political corruption in the Ottoman Empire was widespread, regional conflicts and rebellions tore at the nation, and the failure to industrialize had left the Ottomans far behind European countries like Great Britain and France.

## Early Reform Effort

When Sultan Selim III took the Ottoman throne in 1778, he set about reforming the state. He realized the disadvantages of his outdated army and asked French military advisors to come and help modernize Ottoman arms and tactics. (A young officer named Napoleon Bonaparte was slated to fill one position, but days before he was scheduled to leave for Istanbul, Napoleon got caught up in military affairs in Paris. He would eventually lead France to conquer much of Europe and parts of Africa.)

With the help of the European instructors, the Ottoman military did improve and adopt modern weapons and tactics. Perhaps the most influential military advisor to the Ottomans was Baron Francois de Tott, a French aristocrat who helped to establish a training school called the Naval Mathematical College during the 1770s. However, even de Tott achieved only limited success in helping the Ottomans, partly because of their distrust of outsiders.

Ottoman governors in the farthest reaches of the empire were unhappy about the improvements to the sultan's army. The provincial rulers had become quite independent, and feared that Selim III would use his newly trained forces to enforce his authority. They stirred up rebellion among the sultan's elite forces, the Janissaries, who had always enjoyed a great degree of independence. Initially, unrest among the Janissaries compelled the government to delay further reforms. In 1807, however, the elite corps staged a revolt and deposed Selim III, placing his nephew Mustafa IV on the throne.

When loyalists who believed in Selim's reforms marched on Istanbul, Mustafa IV had the former sultan executed. The new sultan hoped this would undermine the loyalists' cause. They were not deterred, however, and deposed Mustafa in 1808, leaving his brother, Mahmud II (1808–39), to rule.

Sultan Mahmud II lived in constant fear of being assassinated or losing control. He tried to squash any threat to his power early and thoroughly. On June 7, 1826, Mahmud II disbanded the Janissaries and replaced them with a new militia that was controlled by the state and not the local lords. The elite forces rioted and threatened to overtake the capital, but the sultan had popular support and a strong, well-trained army, so the rioting Janissaries were soon defeated. Mahmud II then deprived local leaders of their right to arrange for their own hereditary successors, thus making the regional governors a direct extension of the central government. This move, along with the military reforms, rid the state of much corruption and moved the Ottoman Empire toward a modern system of government.

This page from an Austrian book published in the late 17th century shows a commander of Janissaries, the Ottoman sultan's elite fighting force. In 1807 the Janissaries revolted and removed the reforming Sultan Selim III.

## Greek Rebellion

While Mahmud II pressed for reform within the empire, the Orthodox Christians of Greece pushed for independence from the Ottoman Empire. In 1821, the Greeks began their revolution, gaining support from Russia and other European nations. A secret Greek nationalist society, the Philiki Hetairia (Society of Friends) took hold in Istanbul. When Mahmud found out about it, he imprisoned Greek bishops and pressured the Orthodox Church to condemn Philiki Hetairia, but these measures only fanned the flames of revolution.

Over the next few months, the Ottoman army tried to put down the rebellion that arose in the Greek lands. Greek Christian populations were often murdered in areas where Muslims dominated; in retaliation, the insurgents attacked Muslims living on the fringes of the Greek lands. Eventually, the Ottomans could no longer maintain order in the Balkan Peninsula. Their troops holed up in strongholds while the revolutionaries swarmed across the land.

When the Greek leaders began feuding amongst themselves, a civil war broke out in the Balkan Peninsula. Seeing an opportunity to suppress the divided revolutionaries, Mahmud II called upon Muhammad Ali, the viceroy of the Ottoman territory of Egypt, for aid. Muhammad Ali sent an army under the command of his son Ibrahim to crush the Greek rebellion. The sultan promised Ibrahim that he could govern the islands of Crete and the Peloponnese peninsula if the Greeks were defeated. Ibrahim's army was quite effective in terrorizing and ravaging the Greek lands. Over the next five years, the Greeks suffered under the Egyptian onslaught.

British, French, and Russian warships destroy the Ottoman and Egyptian fleets at the decisive Battle of Navarino, October 1827. The Ottoman defeat in the Greek War of Independence (1821–1829) marked the first time that a national group subject to Turkish rule had gained its freedom, and inspired other nationalities to seek independence.

In 1826, the tide tuned. A small band of Greeks defeated a besieging Egyptian army at the city of Mani. In the following year, the Ottoman navy was overcome by a combined fleet of British, French, and Russian ships at Navarino. With foreign aid, the Greek land forces pushed the Ottomans out of the Peloponnese peninsula. By 1830 Greece had gained its independence from the Ottoman Empire.

## War with Egypt

With nothing to show for having helped the sultan, in 1831 Muhammad Ali decided to break Egypt away from the Ottoman Empire. Mahmud II was unable to get Muhammad Ali back under control by himself. In 1833, he had to ask Russia, France, and Britain—his recent enemies—to help him tame his former ally. Outnumbered, Muhammad Ali agreed to a French proposal that he would remain governor of Egypt and Crete, and his son, Ibrahim, would become governor of Damascus and Aleppo (cities that are part of present-day Syria) as well as Adana (a city in modern Turkey). Muhammad Ali and Ibrahim also agreed to remain under Ottoman suzerainty, a diplomatic relationship in which a region remains under the control of a larger state but is granted limited autonomy in exchange for tribute in the form of money or goods.

Muhammad Ali restarted the Turko-Egyptian War in 1839 and routed Mahmud's forces at the decisive Battle of Nezib, in Turkey, on June 24. Mahmud II died on July 1 of that year, and his teenage son Abdulmecid I (1839–61) took power. Abdulmecid was too young and inexperienced to handle a threat-

Muhammad Ali, the Ottoman viceroy of Egypt, went to war against the sultan's forces twice, eventually winning the right for his descendants to rule Egypt after his death.

ened Egyptian attack on Istanbul, so Great Britain rescued the Ottomans by blocking Egyptian naval access to Istanbul. British ships then bombarded parts of Egypt, forcing Muhammad Ali to end hostilities.

## The Tanzimat Reforms

With the crisis temporarily averted, Abdulhamid I issued the Gulhane Decree, or "noble rescript of the Rose Court." This decree promised Christians, Jews, and other non-Muslims living within the Ottoman Empire freedom of religion, a reasonable tax structure, equality before the law, and the right to live free of persecution. This marked the start of the Tanzimat ("reorganization") reforms. Besides providing some civil rights, these social reforms created updated schools, hospitals, and a legal code that was separate from Islamic holy law. The Tanzimat Era lasted

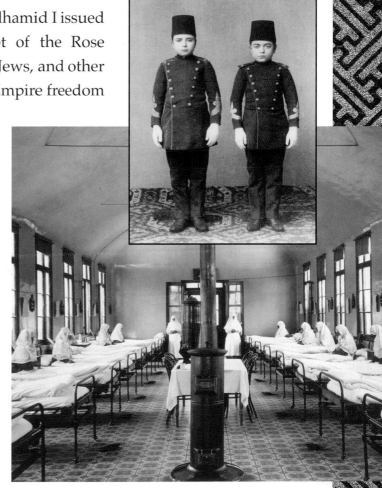

During the Tanzimat period, many new hospitals, schools, and other public buildings were constructed. (Top) Uniformed students at a military middle school in Edirne. (Right) The tuberculosis ward of the Hasköy Hospital for women, Istanbul.

through the reign of Abdulmecid I and his successor, Abdulaziz, who ruled from 1861 to 1876.

One thing the Tanzimat sultans failed to address was how to resolve the Egyptian troubles. In 1882, during a multinational conference that Sultan Abdulhamid II (ruled 1876–1909) refused to attend, it was decided that British troops would occupy Egypt to keep peace. The British also wanted to control Egypt because of the Suez Canal, which was a vital route for British shipping to and from its colonies in Asia, such as British India. Although the Ottomans were still technically rulers of Egypt, in reality their influence in that area was over.

Saddled with war costs and the price of needed reforms, Abdulhamid II had no choice but to address the financial problems of the Ottoman Empire, which had pushed the empire into bankruptcy shortly before his reign began. In 1881, he agreed to the formation of the Council of Public Debt, made up of European bankers who administered Ottoman moneys and tried to help the empire develop new export businesses. The weakening empire was now more reliant than ever on foreign assistance.

## Losing the Balkan States

In 1875, at the same time the sultan's government was instituting the Tanzimat reforms and ignoring the troubles in its Egyptian territories, Orthodox Christian peasants in the Balkans (present-day southeastern Europe, named for the Balkan Mountains in Bulgaria) rebelled against Ottoman rule. They turned to Russia for help, and Russia declared war on Turkey in 1877. By 1878, this Russo-Turkish War, one of many throughout the history of the Ottoman Empire, was nearly over, with the Russian forces threatening Istanbul. The Turks were forced to sign the Treaty of San Stefano in March 1878. The agreement gave independence to Serbia, Montenegro, and Romania. It also contained terms for a new "Big Bulgaria," made up not only of present-day Bulgaria, but also the Aegean coast and Macedonia. The European powers, worried about the threat of "Big Bulgaria," trimmed it down again to its former size with the Treaty of Berlin in July 1878.

Abdulhamid II was not even invited to the table for the Treaty of Berlin. Although Macedonia remained an Ottoman possession, Bulgaria became semi-independent and was placed under Russian influence. Great Britain received the former Ottoman island of Cyprus, and Austria-Hungary was granted authority to manage the foreign affairs of Bosnia-Herzegovina.

## The Young Ottomans

As the empire crumbled, the old political order also rotted in the heart of Istanbul. In the mid-1860s, a group of intellectuals had begun reacting against the bureaucracy that resulted from the Tanzimat reforms and the centralization of power in the hands of the sultan. This group was known as the Young

By using harsh tactics to crush nationalist movements, Sultan Abdulhamid II (1842–1918) managed to prevent the breakup of the Ottoman Empire in the late 19th century.

The entrance to the Sublime Porte ("lofty gate"), where the grand vizier and other high-ranking Ottoman officials had their offices. This photo was taken a few years after the protests at the Porte that led to the Young Ottoman constitution.

Ottomans, and they wanted a parliamentary government and liberal political reforms that would eliminate much of the bureaucratic power structure. They advocated a return to Islamic principles of communal government, in which the sultan sought counsel from the people. Such views, however, were understandably rejected by the sultan and the bureaucratic elite, and several Young Ottomans were forced into European exile. Those that remained could not form a political front, and by the 1870s the organization fell apart.

Though not all of the Young Ottomans' ideas were well received, progressive reformers in the 1870s clung to the notion that a constitutional government might help the empire overcome the financial and political troubles that had been made worse by the combination of bureaucracy and autocracy. In 1876 a group of students rioted in front of the Sublime Porte, where the sultan and his advisors held court. They threatened to hang the grand vizier, Mahmud Nedim, if the government would not undertake reform. The students demanded that the sultan give up his supreme authority and allow the creation of a constitution and a parliament to check his power.

The protests succeeded because many Turkish statesmen had come to see the wisdom of the Young Ottomans' point of view and sided with the demonstrators. The grand vizier was replaced, and one of the Young Ottoman leaders, Midhat Pasha, was appointed to the sultan's council of advisors (the divan).

Abdulhamid II, who came to power soon after the Young Ottoman uprising, initially seemed to cooperate with the Young Ottomans. The Ottoman Constitution was drawn up in 1876, and Midhat Pasha was named Abdulhamid II's grand vizier. The constitution provided for two houses of parliament. However, this provision was immediately undermined. The document defined the sultan as infallible because he was the caliph, the religious leader of the Islamic state, and Abdulhamid insisted on a provision stating that he could suspend the constitution and dissolve the parliament at any time. Abdulhamid exercised this provision on February 14, 1878. The suspended Ottoman parliament would not meet again for three decades. Just as the liberal idealism of the Young Ottomans had seemingly found a place in Ottoman law, the reformists allowed the power of the sultan to sweep it aside.

Abdulhamid was an absolute monarch, but he did permit some changes that modernized the Ottoman Empire. The Hejaz Railway, which ran from Damascus to the important city of Medina on the Arabian Peninsula, was completed in 1908. Although the Hejaz Railway was designed to carry religious pilgrims to Medina, it was also a means for Abdulhamid II to move troops into, and thus control, a formerly remote area of his empire.

## The Young Turk Revolution

Despite taking some measures to modernize the Ottoman empire, Abdulhamid II ruled with an iron hand. He had a secret police force that severely punished any real or imagined threat to his sovereignty. The sultan was also far removed from the everyday life of Istanbul and the larger empire, interacting only with palace officials.

Some younger Ottoman subjects who had been educated in Europe believed that the sultanate was no longer relevant to the rest of the world. They sought to restore the constitution and abolish the bureaucracy that created special privileges for government officials. The new generation of reformers were called the Young Turks in honor of their predecessors, the Young Ottomans. The Young Turks were made up of artists, intellectuals, political activists, soldiers, and many other disenchanted professionals.

The Young Turks and other interest groups wanting change established the Committee of Union and Progress (CUP) in 1907. The Committee of Union and Progress envisioned a unified Turkish nation governed by elected representatives and a permanent parliament. The Young Turks did not entirely share this vision, as they wished to retain the position of sultan, making the empire a constitutional monarchy.

In the summer of 1908, Ottoman army officers stationed in Macedonia revolted, demanding that Abdulhamid II restore the constitution of 1876.

Fearing that his army would march on Istanbul, the sultan declared that the Ottoman Constitution would be put back into effect on July 24. He also disbanded his secret police force and promised to convene an elected parliament within three months, which he did. The CUP won less than a quarter of the parliament seats in November 1908, but other reform groups also took their place in this legislature. The Ciragan Palace became the new hall of parliament.

In February 1909 Young Turks in control of the Committee of Union and Progress ousted the grand vizier, Mehmed Kamil Pasha, who opposed the Young Turk reforms. They replaced him with Huseyin Hilmi, who was sympathetic to their cause. The Young Turks also began promoting women's rights and encouraged women to appear in public without the veil that Islamic tradition required them to wear.

## The Countercoup

In April 1909 religious students and sympathetic Ottoman soldiers staged a counterrevolution, demanding that the Committee of Union and Progress be abolished. They wanted a new government to restore full authority to the sultan. Traditionalist protesters broke into the parliament hall and killed two CUP officials.

Sultan Abdulhamid II took the opportunity to stir up popular revolt against the radical ideas of the Committee of Union and Progress and make a bid to reinstate his authority. He appointed a grand vizier and quickly put together a traditional divan to replace the CUP parliament. He courted the conservative elements of the empire and those who wanted to keep Islamic law as the basis for government and legal decisions in the empire. With this power base, he staged a countercoup with support from military units in the capital.

Members of the Ottoman parliament were forced to flee from Istanbul. An army general named Mahmud Shevket Pasha, who supported the goals of the Committee of Union and Progress, dispatched one of his junior officers, Mustafa Kemal, along with army units that had been stationed in the Balkans, to protect the legislators. The reformers in parliament reconvened at San Stefano, a village to the west of Istanbul.

Creating unity between the defenders of parliament and the strong military forces from the empire's fringes gave the reform elements enough strength to put down the sultan's countercoup. Abdulhamid II reinstated parliament in hopes that the gesture would keep him in power. It was too late, however. Parliament asked religious leaders for a *fatwa* (in Turkish, *fetva*), or Islamic legal ruling, ordering his deposition. When the *fatwa* was issued, the 66-year-old sultan fainted at the news that he was to be dethroned and sent into exile. His half-brother Mehmed V became the new sultan on April 27, 1909.

## Turkish Nationalism

Although Abdulhamid II was out of the way, the CUP government still did not operate smoothly. Some officials of the Committee of Union and Progress were more authoritarian than others. The new government revoked freedom of the press once in power, for example, banning the publication of materials that the CUP believed would incite unrest.

The Turkish army leaves Istanbul at the start of the Italo-Turkish War of 1911. Italy easily defeated the Ottomans and captured the North African province of Libya.

Other countries saw a golden opportunity in the Ottoman Empire's bumpy road toward a constitutional monarchy. In 1911 Italy tried to gain control of the Ottomans' North African frontier. The Italo-Turkish War of 1911 was brief, and the Ottomans could do little to defend Libya from Italian conquest. In the fall of 1912, the Balkan League (Greece, Serbia, Montenegro, and newly independent Bulgaria) invaded the Ottoman territories of Macedonia and Thrace. The Balkan League agreed on very little besides their shared hatred of Ottoman rule. However, they won the Balkan War, costing the new sultan all of his territory in Europe except for a narrow strip of land in eastern Thrace.

The military losses made the Committee of Union and Progress less popular, and a rival party called the Liberal Union gained prominence in parliament. The Liberal Union Party was an offshoot of CUP, but its policies were more tolerant of the ethnic diversity within the empire. It eventually unseated the CUP regime for a brief period in the winter of 1912–13.

Popular sentiment still favored the Committee of Union and Progress, however. The most radical of the Young Turks in the CUP were convinced the problems of the state were evidence that only a strong Turkish nationalism could hold the empire together. In *Empires of the Sand: The Struggle for Mastery in the Middle East 1789–1923*, historians Efraim and Inari Karsh explain:

> All signs of non-Turkic national expression were regarded as treason, and the nationalist societies [i.e. ethnic heritage societies within the various lands of the empire] as a grave threat to Ottoman unity that had to be eradicated, by law or by force.

This ideology would prove disastrous for Armenians and other non-Turkish speaking groups who cherished their own heritage while living in Ottoman lands.

## Rise of the Three Pashas

On January 23, 1913, a throng of CUP members overthrew the Liberal Union, gunning down the minister of war and forcing the grand vizier to resign. At the head of this mob was Ismail Enver, a Young Turk and army general who had fought bravely in the Italo-Turkish War. He appointed himself the new minister of war. Another military man, Ahmed Djemal, became minister of the navy, and a civil servant and CUP member, Mehmed Talat, became minister of the interior. These three powerful figures, who became known as the Three Pashas, essentially ruled the empire for the next six years. Although the Committee of Union and Progress named a new grand vizier, Said Halim, he was not as powerful as the Three Pashas.

The Three Pashas came to power at a turbulent time in world history. A century of peace in Europe was about to end, and the resulting conflict would ultimately spell the end of the Ottoman order.

Ismail Enver was one of three powerful leaders known as the Three Pashas. With Mehmed Talat and Ahmed Djemal, Enver acted as de facto ruler of the Ottoman Empire for six turbulent years, from 1913 to 1918.

# SAVE THE SURVIVORS

**BALTIMORE CITY CAMPAIGN, FEBRUARY 9TH-17TH**

**JOHN E. BOISSEAU,** *Treas.* **119 E. Baltimore St.**

## CAMPAIGN *for* $30,000,000

## AMERICAN COMMITTEE RELIEF IN THE NEAR EAST

### ARMENIA - GREECE - SYRIA - PERSIA

1 MADISON AVE. NEW YORK ~ CLEVELAND H. DODGE. *Treasurer*

The Ottoman Empire entered the First World War in 1914 on the side of the Central Powers. (Right) Entrenched Turkish soldiers await an attack in the Middle East. (Opposite) Ottoman massacres of Armenians and other citizens during the war caused international concern. This poster advertises a fundraiser to help those affected by the conflict.

# 4 *The Ottomans in the First World War*

**W**hen Serbian teenager Gavrilo Princip shot Archduke Franz Ferdinand, the Hapsburg heir to the Austro-Hungarian throne, in Sarajevo, Bosnia, on June 28, 1914, he had no way of knowing that his defiant act in the name of Slavic independence from Austrian rule would initiate a world war. Princip was a Young Bosnian, a group that wanted to free Bosnia-Herzegovina from Austria-Hungary through alliance with Serbia. He wished to liberate the Slavic states, which had labored under

Ottoman rule for centuries before being turned over to Austro-Hungarian control in 1878 at the end of the Russo-Turkic War.

When Austria-Hungary declared war on Serbia in response to the assassination of Franz Ferdinand, Russia defended Serbia, and the rest of Europe was forced to take sides. Germany joined Austria-Hungary to form the Central Powers. Great Britain, France, and Russia drew up an alliance that was known as the Triple Entente. The Ottoman Empire had no clear allegiance at the outset of World War I. Great Britain and France were valuable trading partners, and many Turks wished to retain this economic advantage. However, Ismail Enver, the CUP's minister of war, thought Germany—with its powerful and well-disciplined military—was sure to win the war, and saw an alliance with Germany as an opportunity to retake the Balkan states and regain a foothold in Europe.

By early August 1914, when war broke out in Europe, Enver and the German ambassador Hans von Wangenheim had already worked out a secret defensive treaty against Russia. As part of the terms of the agreement with von Wangenheim, the Ottomans consented to enter the war only if Germany promised the empire would get island territories in the Aegean back from Greece after a Central Powers victory. More importantly, however, they wanted gold for their treasury before they would join the Central Powers. Wangenheim agreed to these conditions and made other promises as well.

Despite the treaty, the Ottomans publicly declared their neutrality at first. This changed after two German warships, the *Goeben* and the *Breslau*, took refuge in the Bosporus port at Istanbul to escape pursuing British ships. As a neutral power, the Ottomans were required by international law to either send the *Goeben* and *Breslau* back into international waters or to deactivate them for the rest of the conflict. Instead, the Ottoman government took possession of the ships, pretending to have purchased them. German Admiral Wilhelm Souchon remained in command of the vessels, but the warships were renamed the *Yavuz Sultan Selim* and *Medilli* and put into Ottoman service.

The Ottomans continued their pretense of neutrality for the first three months of the war. However, tensions with the Triple Entente rose in late September, when the Ottomans closed the Dardanelles, blocking Russian ships from entering or leaving the Black Sea. On October 28, 1914, the *Yavuz Sultan Selim* and *Medilli* attacked the Russian ports of Odessa and Sebastopol on the Black Sea. The Ottoman Empire issued an unconvincing apology, blaming the Germans who had manned the ships. Russia declared war on the Ottoman Empire on November 4. Great Britain

Ahmed Djemal (left), one of the Three Pashas, stands with a German officer. The Three Pashas decided to align the Ottoman Empire with Germany in hopes of regaining some of the empire's lost territory.

The German warships *Breslau* (left) and *Goeben* (right) are anchored in the harbor at Istanbul. After the ships shelled Russia's Black Sea ports in October 1914, the Allies declared war on the Ottoman Empire.

and France followed suit the next day. All pretense of Ottoman neutrality was gone.

## Early Campaigns

It took several months for the Ottoman government to mobilize a fighting force of about 800,000 men. Enver, anxious to regain the empire's lost glory, set out on a poorly planned invasion of Russia during late December 1914. The drive into the Caucasus Mountains was beset by problems, including a harsh winter and lack of communication. At the decisive Battle of Sarikamish, the Russians routed the Ottomans, costing Ismail Enver close to 85,000 troops. He slunk back to Istanbul in early 1915, blaming the Germans for providing no assistance.

Ahmed Djemal, the Ottoman minister of the navy, did not fare much better. He attacked the Suez Canal in Egypt on February 2, 1915, only to retreat quickly in the face of British military might. The defeat was made more embarrassing by Djemal's boastful words beforehand: he had vowed to "rescue" Egypt from Britain or die trying.

While the Ottomans were unable to stage a successful offensive, they did manage to thwart an invasion of the empire by the Triple Entente. In the winter of 1914–15, the Allies were anxious to open up the Dardanelles and the Bosporus so military supplies could be shipped to Russia. They devised a strategy calling for British troops to land on the Gallipoli peninsula in Thrace and advance into the surrounding hills. A successful landing would create a staging area for an Allied drive on Istanbul, which would force the Ottoman Empire out of the war.

On March 18, 1915, British and French ships entered the Dardanelles in hopes that a naval attack might secure control of the waterway. However, they found the straits well defended. Several warships struck mines that the Ottomans had placed in the straits, and artillery rained down on the Allied ships from the surrounding hills. The fleet was forced to retire with considerable losses.

Turkish soldiers fend off an attack in the hills above the Dardanelles strait, 1915. The Ottoman army successfully defended the Gallipoli Peninsula from invasion, forcing the Allied force (mainly British) to retreat after suffering heavy losses.

On April 24, the British navy tried again, this time escorting the landing force to the beaches of Gallipoli. The troops made it ashore, but the coastline was lined with Ottoman guns, stopping the move inland. An Ottoman commander named Mustafa Kemal used the high ground to his advantage. The fighting raged into the hot summer, and many of the Allies fell ill with disease. After Kemal's soldiers repelled a final strong push by the British in

Zealand troops in August 1915, it was clear to British leaders that they did not have enough strength to dislodge the defenders. In December 1915, after suffering more than 140,000 men killed or wounded in the disastrous campaign, the British began pulling their troops out of the Gallipoli peninsula.

Gallipoli had failed to knock the Ottoman Empire out of World War I. The Three Pashas still controlled the Black Sea and the straits. The Ottomans also succeeded in repelling British attacks in the region known as Mesopotamia (modern-day Iraq) in 1915 and 1916, gaining a major victory at Kut.

## Conflict Within the Empire

But even as Ottoman leaders reveled in their victories, nationalist unrest within the empire was beginning to undermine Ottoman strength. The desire of various nationalities living within the empire to rule themselves had been a problem for many years. The Committee of Union and Progress had tried to eliminate these groups' traditional languages and cultures and impose a Turkish identity on all subjects of the empire. This led to resentment and widespread resistance.

The Ottomans dealt particularly harshly with the nationalist aspirations of one group under their control, the Armenians. At the outbreak of the war roughly 2 million people of Armenian descent lived within the Ottoman Empire. Most lived in Turkish Armenia, a group of *vilayets* in Eastern Anatolia, which bordered the Russian Empire. Most Armenians were Christian, adhering to Gregorian, Orthodox, or Protestant beliefs, and were proud of their ethnic and linguistic heritage.

During the reign of Sultan Abdulhamid II, secret Armenian societies had begun to agitate for independence from the Ottoman Empire, often resorting to terrorist attacks to draw attention to their demands. One Armenian group nearly succeeded in assassinating the sultan on July 21, 1905. Such acts brought swift retribution, however. The sultan's military would routinely search villages in Turkish Armenia looking for conspirators and rebels. Armenians suspected of being traitors were swiftly executed.

When the CUP government came to power, Armenians were forbidden to speak their native language in public. The government in Istanbul persecuted those who dissented. Neighboring Russia offered support to the Ottoman Armenians, and some Armenians joined the ranks of the Russian army to fight against the Turks in World War I. Ottoman leaders used this connection as an excuse to rid the empire of Armenians who might cause trouble during the war. In May 1915 the Committee of Union and Progress ordered the deportation of Armenians to camps in the Syrian desert along the Euphrates River.

The stated purpose of this order was to keep the Armenians from aiding the Russian armies, which were advancing through the Caucasus region toward the Ottoman border. However, many deportees were killed before the journey even began. Some of the rest were crammed into trains like cattle and sent southward, or simply marched to the labor camps. The deportation decree stated that the Armenians were supposed to be fed and protected on the journey. Instead, Turkish soldiers starved many Armenians and allowed others to be beaten or murdered by locals along the way. After the difficult and dangerous journey, hard labor awaited those who made it to the desert encampments.

Violence against Armenians living in the Ottoman Empire spiked in 1915, after the Three Pashas ordered Armenians to be deported from their homes. The bodies of massacred Armenians lie outside a building in Aleppo, Syria.

At the same time, Armenian soldiers serving in the Ottoman army were disarmed. Some were executed, while others were forced to join labor battalions.

Representatives of many foreign governments, including the United States (which had not yet become involved in the First World War), reported massacres and atrocities committed on the orders of the Ottoman government. In July 1915 the American ambassador to the empire, Henry Morgenthau Sr., sent a telegram to Washington, D.C., in which he alerted U.S. leaders about the problem. "Deportation of and excesses against

American ambassador Henry Morganthau (wearing dark hat), who warned the U.S. government about the massacre of Armenians in the empire, is surrounded by Armenian refugees in Athens.

peaceful Armenians is increasing and from harrowing reports of eye witnesses it appears that a campaign of race extermination is in progress under a pretext of reprisal against rebellion," he wrote. In September 1915, another American diplomat, Leslie Davis, reported finding the corpses of thousands of dead Armenians in the area around Lake Göeljuk. However, despite such evidence of the Ottoman government's systematic plan to exterminate the Armenians, Western governments were unwilling to step in and halt the atrocities.

Estimates of the number of Armenians killed by the Ottomans between 1915 and 1918 vary from 600,000 (according to the Turkish government) to more than 1.2 million (a figure accepted by many Western historians). These figures also include thousands of Kurdish and Assyrian peoples who were swept up in the tragedy.

# The Arab Revolt

In another part of the Ottoman Empire, a nationalist insurrection had a very different outcome. In 1916 Sharif Hussein ibn Ali, the Ottoman governor of Mecca and the Hejaz (the northwestern region of present-day Saudi Arabia), declared himself king of the Arabs and called for a revolution against Ottoman rule. Great Britain and France supported the sharif, seeing his revolt as another way to pressure the Ottoman Empire. In a series of letters exchanged during 1915 and 1916 with Sir Arthur Henry McMahon, the British high commissioner in Egypt, Hussein had agreed to fight the Ottomans in exchange for Allied support of his Arab state.

The British army sent a military advisor named T. E. Lawrence to the Hejaz. Lawrence of Arabia, as he came to be known, was widely respected by the Arabs with whom he fought. Lawrence encouraged the Arab army to destroy parts of the Hejaz Railway, which would make it harder for Ottoman troops to travel easily to the Hejaz. Constantly guarding the rails and repairing the vandalism distracted the Ottoman army, tying down troops that could have helped the empire's war effort elsewhere.

When the Arabs cut Ottoman supply lines, Turkish troops had to vacate the city of Aqaba in July 1917. The British then used this port as a base of operations in the region, providing arms and ammunition to the Arabs. British troops also marched from Egypt to attack Ottoman strongholds, working with the Arabs. In December 1917, the British captured Jerusalem, one of the most important cities of the region.

## The End of the Ottoman Empire

The Three Pashas received good news in late 1917, when word came that the Bolsheviks, led by Vladimir Lenin, had seized power in Russia. The new Bolshevik government pulled Russia out of the war, signing the Treaty of Brest-Litovsk. Under the terms of the treaty, Russia gave the Ottomans back some of the territory it had seized during the 1877–78 Russo-Turkish War. The armistice also relieved pressure on the eastern front, allowing the Ottomans to focus their energies elsewhere.

However, by 1918 the Ottoman government could no longer afford to continue the war. The Three Pashas were willing to accept U.S. President Woodrow Wilson's proposal for a peace settlement that would allow residents of the empire who were not Turkish to form their own sovereign nations if Istanbul was granted some authority over Turkish parts of the Middle East. That became increasingly unlikely, however, as Ottoman forces suffered more defeats during 1918. In September British forces commanded by General Edmund Allenby defeated the Ottoman Army at the Battle of Megiddo, and on October 1 Damascus fell to Allenby's soldiers.

Unable to cope with the losses in men and territory, the Ottoman government capitulated. The 36th and final sultan, Mehmed VI (ruled 1918–22), sent his naval minister to Mudros, a Greek port on the island of Lemnos. The Allies were represented by a British admiral named Somerset Calthorpe. On October 30, 1918, the two sides signed the Armistice of Mudros.

Turkish soldiers captured by British forces in the Middle East, 1918. On October 30 of that year, the sultan's representatives signed the Armistice of Mudros, which ended the empire's part in the First World War.

The war itself did not last much longer. Austria-Hungary collapsed at the end of October, and less than two weeks later, on November 11, 1918, Germany signed an armistice with the Allies.

Within days of the armistice, Istanbul was occupied by Allied troops and its harbor was filled with Allied warships. Admiral Calthorpe was placed in charge of managing the international affairs of what was left of the empire—primarily the Anatolian Peninsula. The evidence of mass killings of Armenians during the war horrified the Allies. The Three Pashas—who had conducted the war and ordered the killings of Armenians—became hunted war criminals. They fled the capital and boarded a ship for Germany. Mehmed Talat and Ahmed Djemal were later assassinated by Armenians seeking to avenge the massacres, while Ismail Enver was killed by soldiers of the Russian Red Army while trying to stir a Turkish rebellion in the Central Asian area that is now Tajikistan. The Ottoman Empire was no more. Its territories waited to be divided up among the victors.

After the end of the First World War, Turkish nationalists battled the Allies to establish a new state. (Opposite) Mustafa Kemal (seated, third from left) and members of the Grand National Assembly in Sivas, 1919. (Right) The delegates to Lausanne, including Ismet Pasha (seated, fourth from left), negotiated the borders of modern Turkey in 1923.

# 5 New Nation-States in the Middle East

Istanbul was cold and demoralized in the winter of 1918–19. Allied warships anchored in the Golden Horn served as a constant reminder of defeat. Allied leaders were repulsed by evidence of the slaughter of Greek, Assyrian, and Armenian Christians, which the Ottomans tried to blame on the chaos of war. The Ottomans had also misled the Allies about their neutrality at the start of the war. Many among the Allies thought such deception and murder should not go unpunished. Others wanted to forgive these acts in hopes of creating strong allies when the empire was broken apart.

## Greece Invades Western Anatolia

Sensing the Allies' uncertainty, Greece attempted to lay claim to parts of the western Ottoman Empire. These regions had significant Greek populations, and Greek Prime Minister Elefthérious Venizélos envisioned Istanbul as the capital of a new Greek empire. Venizélos cited the massacre of Greek and Armenian Christians as evidence that the Ottoman Turks were inferior leaders who had never had the best interests of the empire's non-Turkish people at heart. He argued that Ottoman Greeks should be liberated from Turkish rule. On May 15, 1919, Greek ships landed in the Anatolian port town of Smyrna with Allied support.

Mustafa Kemal, the Ottoman hero of Gallipoli, was in Anatolia under the sultan's orders to collect arms and demobilize what was left of Ottoman forces there. Instead, he encouraged the Turkish people to resist the Greek invasion of Smyrna. The resulting battle did not go well for the Turks, however, and once the Greeks routed the defenders, many Greeks and Christian citizens persecuted and humiliated the defeated Muslims in the city.

Dreaming of a Greek empire, Prime Minister Elefthérios Venizélos (1864–1936) ordered Greek forces to invade East Thrace and Ionia (the region around Smyrna).

## Two Governments in Anatolia

By July 1919 Kemal had resigned from the military and redirected his energies toward forming a new representative government in Anatolia. The sultan's government ordered that he be arrested and executed, but Kemal had declared himself a free citizen of Erzerum who was no longer under the authority of Istanbul. Kemal and his fellow Turkish nationalists met first in Erzerum, then again in Sivas. In December, the Turkish nationalists' new parliament, called the Grand National Assembly met in Ankara, the newly declared capital of the nationalist movement. Now, the Allies had to contend with two Turkish governments: the old Ottoman regime in Istanbul and the nationalist government in Ankara.

On March 16, 1920, British and French troops seized the old capital, Istanbul. In a gesture to show his occupiers that there would be no rebellion in the former empire, the compliant Sultan Mehmed VI dissolved the Ottoman parliament for the third and final time.

In Ankara the Grand National Assembly convened on April 23 and elected Mustafa Kemal its president. In June Kemal's troops tried to storm Istanbul to free it from Allied occupation. Although Kemal did not acknowledge Mehmed VI's authority, he did not want foreigners occupying the ancient Turkish capital either.

Kemal's attempt to liberate Istanbul failed, and the Allies refused to include his nationalist government in any negotiations over the future of the empire. In particular, the British government supported the sultan, although some British diplomats were beginning to see that Mehmed VI was not the man to head the government of a new Turkey.

The government of Mehmed VI grudgingly signed the Treaty of Sevres on August 10, 1920, to officially end its involvement in World War I. The treaty, based on talks held among representatives of the Allies in San Remo during April 1920, was a bitter pill for the Ottoman Turks. It officially abolished the Ottoman Empire. Turkey lost its territories in Asia and North Africa. Armenia and Kurdistan, Ottoman holdings near the Russian border, would now rule themselves, and Greece would get control over the Aegean islands near the Dardanelles strait, gateway to the Mediterranean Sea. Under the Treaty of Sevres, foreigners would again be able to conduct business in Turkey without paying taxes. Furthermore, the treaty limited the size of the Turkish armed forces to no more than 50,000 troops.

## Disappointment in the Middle East

The Turks were not the only people unhappy with the way the Ottoman Empire was carved up. While some national groups, such as the Armenians, gained their freedom, other groups, such as the Arabs, essentially traded Ottoman control for rule by the Allies.

Sharif Hussein had launched the Arab Revolt in 1916 because he believed, based on his correspondence with the British diplomat Arthur Henry McMahon, that he would gain control over a region stretching from modern-day Israel to Iraq. Unbeknownst to the sharif, British and French leaders had other ideas. In May 1916 they had secretly signed the Sykes-Picot Agreement (named for the diplomats who had negotiated the arrangement, Britain's Mark Sykes and France's Francois Georges-Picot), which divided the Arab lands into a patchwork of territories that these two countries would largely control at war's end.

According to the Sykes-Picot Agreement, the Allies would divide the Middle East into spheres of influence. France was to control Syria (which then included most of modern-day Lebanon), the northern part of Iraq, and the southern Anatolian Peninsula, while Britain got the rest of Iraq, Palestine, Transjordan, and the western Arabian Peninsula. While he was helping shape the agreement, Sykes was unaware of his countryman McMahon's promises to Sharif Hussein. T.E. Lawrence was also unaware that the Arabs were to be cheated out of the sovereignty they fought so hard to attain. After the war Lawrence attempted unsuccessfully to persuade British diplomats that Arab independence—not British domination—would be more useful to British interests in the future.

Thwarted in their quest for independence, many Arabs resented the actions of Britain and France. Arab leaders were further angered when they learned about the Balfour declaration, a British policy statement that endorsed the creation of a Jewish state in Palestine. In November 1917, British Foreign Secretary Arthur James Balfour had sent a letter to Baron Edmund de Rothschild, a member of a family of prominent financiers and a leader in the Jewish community of Great Britain. The letter said that the British cabinet supported the establishment of a Jewish homeland in Palestine, as long as its creation did not infringe on the rights of the Arabs who already lived in the region. Zionists, who had been pushing for such a homeland since the 19th century, rejoiced at this promise. Part of Britain's motive for creating a Jewish homeland was to drum up support for the Allied cause and to get the United States—which had a large Jewish population—to join the war on behalf of the Allies.

The Allies ignored Arab demands for independence at the 1919 Paris Peace Conference. In Paris, creation of the League of Nations gave the Allies a mechanism through which they could legally control the development of the Middle East. The League, which was dominated by Britain and France, granted mandates to the victorious Allied powers, giving them authority to oversee the internal and international affairs of newly created countries. As the Sykes-Picot Agreement had spelled out, Britain and France each shared control over the newly formed Arab states.

Sharif Hussein and his sons were granted a measure of power in the new Arab states. Faisal was chosen by the Arabs to rule the region known as Syria.

The Arab leader Faisal, son of Sharif Hussein of Mecca, poses for a photo at the 1919 Paris Peace Conference. British officer T. E. Lawrence is pictured standing behind and to the right of Faisal. Arab hopes for an independent state stretching across the Middle East were dashed at the conference, although the British later made Faisal king of Iraq.

Another son, Abdullah, became king of Transjordan (the modern state of Jordan). Sharif Hussein and his son Ali were to rule a territory on the western Arabian Peninsula known as the Hejaz.

Things did not work out exactly as the Allies had intended, however. When the League of Nations gave France the mandate for Syria, Faisal was forced out as ruler, and the British installed him as king of Iraq in 1921. On the Arabian Peninsula, the powerful Saud family, longtime rivals of Sharif Hussein's Hashemite clan, went to war against the ruler. The British did little to support their former ally, and by 1927 they had recognized Abd al-Aziz ibn Saud as the king of the Hejaz. (Abd al-Aziz eventually extended his control over most of the peninsula, and in 1932 renamed his kingdom for his family, Saudi Arabia.) Today, Jordan is the only country that still has a Hashemite ruler.

Although the British gained control over the region known as Palestine, where the Jewish people wanted to establish their homeland, the British stalled on Lord Balfour's promise to establish a Jewish state. Both Jewish and Arab residents of Palestine were unhappy with British rule during the mandate period, and violence was a common problem.

## The Turkish War of Independence

The harsh terms of the Treaty of Sevres united the Turks against the foreign occupiers. Mustafa Kemal and other Ottoman officers organized resistance and began a series of wars against the Greeks, Italians, and Armenians. Known collectively as the Turkish War of Independence, the fighting lasted from May 1919 to October 1922.

The Armenians had been promised their own state at the 1919 Paris Peace Conference, and by signing the Treaty of Sevres the sultan had promised to respect Armenian independence. The Democratic Republic of Armenia, formed in May 1920, included territory in the eastern Anatolian Peninsula as well as part of Russian Armenia. However, both the Russians and Kemal's nationalists immediately began military campaigns to recapture the territory. Over the next few months Armenia was squeezed between the Turks and the Russians.

U.S. President Woodrow Wilson was asked to intervene by accepting the League of Nations mandate for Armenia, which would have offered protection to the tiny state. However, after the First World War most people in the United States were opposed to further involvement in foreign affairs, and Congress rejected this appeal.

By December 1920 the Democratic Republic of Armenia had collapsed. Its territory was divided between Turkey and the Union of Soviet Socialist Republics (U.S.S.R.), which had taken over control of the former Russian Empire after the czar was overthrown in 1917. In 1921 the Turkish nationalists made a treaty with the Soviet Union that established the border between the two countries.

Like the Armenians, Kurds would continue to live under the rule of others. The Treaty of Sevres had also promised the Kurds their own state, but when the Turkish nationalists recaptured control of the northern Kurdish territory the Allies refused to press for Kurdish independence. Instead, control over other parts of the region known as Kurdistan was assigned to the new mandate states of Iraq and Syria.

Encountering unexpectedly strong resistance from the Turkish nationalists, the French and the Italians withdrew from Anatolia in the fall of 1921. However, Greek leaders continued to pursue their dream of control over the peninsula. The decisive clash between the Turkish nationalists and the Greeks was the Battle of Dumlupinar, which began on August 26, 1922, and ended on September 9. It was a decisive Turkish victory, with Mustafa Kemal leading his men on the attack. They drove the Greeks out of the port of Smyrna, but not before fires destroyed much of the city. Allied ships were used to evacuate Greek soldiers and citizens to safety.

Surprised by the resistance by the nationalist army, Great Britain was no longer willing to continue supporting the Greek bid for empire. The British ambassador Sir Horace Rumbold met with the Turkish nationalists in Mudanya to negotiate an end to the fighting. The Armistice of Mudanya, signed on October 11, 1922, restored Greek borders to their pre-World War I state. The nationalists agreed to let the British remain in the Dardanelles region—and the capital—until a new agreement could replace the Treaty of Sevres. The Turks, however, demanded that all other foreign powers vacate Turkish lands. It was a bold demand, but the Turks had the strength to back it up, leaving the occupiers little choice but to consent.

## The Treaty of Lausanne

Two weeks after the Mudanya accord was signed, the Allies invited representatives from both the Istanbul and Ankara governments to Lausanne, Switzerland, to negotiate a new treaty more acceptable to the former empire.

Mehmed VI (1861–1926) was the 36th and final sultan of the Ottoman Empire. With the nationalist victory, Mehmed VI was forced into exile in November 1922.

Mustafa Kemal was outraged that the Istanbul government was included. He felt that through the nationalists' military success he had proven himself to be the true leader of the Turks. The Grand National Assembly in Ankara formally abolished the Ottoman Empire on the grounds that the sultan's government had folded when the Allies seized Istanbul in 1920. The Ankara government also stated that it would not recognize the sultanate, but that the former sultan could still be the caliph. This meant that although he would have religious authority among Muslims, the sultan would have no say in government affairs.

The Istanbul government quickly caved in to these demands. On November 4, 1922, the sultan's grand vizier and cabinet resigned. Soon after this Mehmed VI climbed aboard a British ship and went into exile, first on the island of Malta, then to San Remo, Italy, where the Allies had originally gathered to decide the Ottoman Empire's fate. His cousin Abdulmecid II was named the new caliph, but by 1924 Kemal's Turkish government had abolished the caliphate. Abdulmecid was given a nominal title of General of the Ottoman Army, and spent most of his later years in Paris.

With the sultanate at an end, Kemal sent a trusted aid, Ismet Pasha, to be Turkey's chief negotiator at Lausanne. Lord Curzon, Great Britain's secretary for foreign affairs, coordinated the talks. After many frustrating starts and stops, the Treaty of Lausanne was finally signed on July 24, 1923. It gave the new nation of Turkey all of Anatolia and part of eastern Thrace. Turkey gave up its claim to several Mediterranean islands, which would be controlled in future by Great Britain, Greece, and Italy. However, the Turks kept the large islands of Imbros and Tenedos at the southern mouth of the Dardanelles. Turkey also gave up any claims to former Ottoman territory in the Middle East, Asia, or North Africa, and the Dardanelles and the Bosporus

Mustafa Kemal Atatürk (1881–1938) is considered the father of modern Turkey. His policies established Turkey as a modern, secular state with a government based on Western democratic principles.

Straits were placed under international control to ensure freedom of movement into the Black Sea. In return, the new Turkey gained complete independence from foreign rule.

The most wrenching condition of the treaty of Lausanne was an agreement between Greece and Turkey to swap portions of their populations. Over a million ethnic Greeks living in Anatolia were forcibly removed from their homes and sent to Greece, while about 500,000 Turks living in Greece were forced to move to Turkey. This caused a great deal of pain and upheaval in the lives of those affected. However, Kemal and other Turkish leaders thought that expelling the Greeks was an important step toward promoting a unified Turkish culture within the new country.

## *The Map Redrawn*

When the Allies left Istanbul, the ancient city was no longer the Turkish capital. Ankara became the capital on October 16, 1923. Kemal declared Turkey to be a republic on October 29, and was elected its first president. He was reelected three times, serving as Turkey's president until his death in 1938.

With the signing of the Treaty of Lausanne, the basic configuration of the modern Middle East had emerged. The non-Turkish subjects of the Ottoman Empire—Arabs, Jews, Armenians, and Kurds—had not gained the complete independence they had been promised. Nor were the new states of the Middle East formed in the way that most people living in the region wished. However, working with the Western powers through the mandate system held out the hope of eventual self-government for Arabs,

Jews, and others. Within half a century the former Ottoman areas of the Middle East had gained their independence. Iraq and the Kingdom of Saudi Arabia became fully independent in 1932, while Jordan, Syria, Lebanon, and Israel gained independence during the 1940s.

Actions and decisions made during and after the First World War continue to have a great impact on modern affairs.

**1280:** Osman I, the first Ottoman sultan, is born.

**1453:** Mehmed II (the Conqueror) seizes the ancient Byzantine capital of Constantinople from Christian forces.

**1520:** Suleiman I, known as "the Magnificent" or "the Lawgiver," gains power. During his reign, which lasts until 1566, he establishes the Ottoman Empire as one of the world's foremost powers.

**1683:** The Second Siege of Vienna fails on September 12. This marks the end of Ottoman expansion and the start of the empire's military decline.

**1703:** The Tulip Era, during the reign of Sultan Ahmed III, is notable for the court's excessive spending at the expense of civic improvement. It ends in 1730.

**1830:** On February 3, Greece wins independence from the Ottoman Empire. This marks the first time that a nationality subject to Ottoman rule successfully gained independence through a revolution.

**1839:** The Noble Rescript promises equality and freedom from harassment to all races and religions living in Ottoman Empire. The Ottomans lose the Turko-Egyptian War.

**1875:** The Balkan League rebels against Ottoman rule. The empire is bankrupt.

**1876:** The Young Ottomans depose Sultan Abdulaziz and draft the Ottoman Constitution of 1876.

**1878:** Sultan Abdulhamid II dissolves parliament and suspends the constitution on February 14.

**1908:** On July 24, the Committee of Union and Progress (CUP) gets the Ottoman constitution restored. Elections are held in November.

**1909:** In April, Muslim traditionalists encouraged by Abdulhamid II stage a counterrevolution. After it fails Abdulhamid II is deposed and sent into exile, and Mehmed V becomes sultan.

**1913:** On January 23, the Three Pashas—Ismail Enver, Mehmed Talat, and Ahmed Djemal—stage a violent coup, transforming the CUP government into a military dictatorship.

**1914:** In August World War I begins in Europe. After many weeks of feigning neutrality, the Ottoman Empire enters on the side of the Central Powers on November 4, 1914.

**1915:** In May the Ottoman government orders that Armenians be deported from their homes near the Russian border, ostensibly to prevent them from assisting an advancing Russian army. This deportation is characterized by wide-scale massacres and abuses of Armenians. In August British and French troops begin a seaborne invasion of the Gallipoli peninsula. After months of fierce fighting the invaders withdraw in December.

**1916:** The Arab Revolt starts in 1916 with Allied support.

**1918:** On October 30 the Ottoman Empire signs the Armistice of Mudros, ending hostilities with the Allies; World War I ends with the signing of an armistice between the Allies and Germany on November 11.

**1919:** Mustafa Kemal organizes nationalist resistance to the Allied forces occupying the Anatolian Peninsula. Clashes between his Turkish troops and Greek, French, Italian, and Armenian forces eventually become known as the Turkish War of Independence.

**1920:** From April 19 to 26 a delegation of Allied leaders meets in San Remo, Italy, to discuss the fate of the Ottoman Empire. On August 10 the sultan's representatives reluctantly sign the Treaty of Sevres, which officially breaks up the empire.

**1922:** On October 11 the Turks sign the Armstice of Mudanya to end the Turkish War of Independence. On November 1 the Grand National Assembly abolishes the sultanate, and 16 days later Sultan Mehmed VI goes into exile.

**1923:** On July 24 Turkey's government signs the Treaty of Lausanne. On October 29, Kemal is elected the first president of Republic of Turkey.

**1924:** The Turkish government officially abolishes the caliphate.

**1938:** Mustafa Kemal Atatürk dies on November 10.

**autocracy**——a government in which authority is held by a single person, such as a monarch.

**caliph**——title given to the Islamic religious leader who is acknowledged to be the successor to the Prophet Muhammad and thus the leader of all Muslims.

**constitutional monarchy**——a form of government which is based on a written constitution but acknowledges an elected or hereditary monarch as the head of state. Unlike a traditional monarchy, in which the ruler has near-absolute power, in a constitutional monarchy the ruler is subject to the restrictions of the constitution.

**divan**——a group of advisors to the sultan who acted as a cabinet and also reviewed legal cases.

**fatwa**——(Turkish: *fetva*) an official ruling issued by an Islamic religious authority and based on Islamic law.

**ideology**——a system of beliefs, values, and ideas that form the basis of a social, economic, or political philosophy or program.

**mandate**——the authority, granted by the League of Nations to an established power like Great Britain or France, to administer a less developed territory. Under the mandate system, the more established countries were expected to help the nation-states formed out of the Ottoman territories after World War I to develop the governmental and social institutions required for stability and independence.

**mosque**——a Muslim house of worship.

**nationalism**——the desire by a group of people with a shared identity and culture for an independent country of their own.

**pasha**——an Ottoman title of respect given to governors, generals, and other high-ranking officials.

*sultan*—a Muslim ruler.

*suzerainty*—a political relationship in which an empire has some control over a territory, but allows local officials to rule its day-to-day affairs in exchange for some form of tribute.

*vilayet*—an Ottoman province, supervised for the sultan by a local governor.

*Zionism*—an international political movement, started during the 19th century, which supported the establishment of a Jewish homeland in the region known as Palestine.

Goodwin, Jason. *Lords of the Horizons*. New York: Henry Holt, 1991.

Harmon, Dan. *Turkey*. Philadelphia: Mason Crest Publishers, 2004.

Lawrence, T.E. *Seven Pillars of Wisdom: A Triumph*. Reprint edition. New York: Anchor, 1991.

Lewis, Bernard. *What Went Wrong?: The Clash Between Islam and Modernity in the Middle East*. New York: Oxford University Press, 2002.

Karsh, Efraim, and Inari Karsh, *Empires of the Sand: The Struggle for Mastery in the Middle East 1789–1923*. Cambridge, Mass.: Harvard University Press, 1999.

Palmer, Alan. *The Decline and Fall of the Ottoman Empire*. New York: Barnes and Noble, 1994.

Wheatcroft, Andrew. *The Ottomans: Dissolving Images*. New York: Penguin, 1995.

## http://www.pbs.org/greatwar

This is a comprehensive Public Broadcasting Service (PBS) Web site about all aspects of World War I. Topics concerning the Ottoman Empire include the Battle of Gallipoli, the accomplishments of Mustafa Kemal, and the massacres of Armenians that began in 1915.

## http://www.turkishembassy.org

This is the Web site of the Turkish Embassy in Washington, D.C. The site includes a basic history of Turkey, as well as interesting photos of the country.

## http://school.discovery.com

This Discovery Channel Web site contains a high-school lesson plan about the Ottoman Empire.

## http://www.allaboutturkey.com

Compiled and written by a native Turkish tour guide, this site contains a great deal of information about the formation of the Republic of Turkey.

## http://www.mq.edu.au/mec/Glossary.html

This is a comprehensive glossary of terms used in Middle Eastern studies from the Centre for Middle East and North African Studies at Macquarie University in Sydney, Australia.

Numbers in **bold italic** refer to captions.

# Index